Mud Kitchens and Beyond

50 exciting ideas for investigative play

Acknowledgements

With thanks to the following for the wonderful mud-kitchen photographs:

The staff and children of The Rainbow Centre, Marham, Norfolk

The staff and children of House of Fun Nursery, Gorleston, Norfolk

Olivia and Fraser Lewis and Ted and Alfie Thompson, who were playing and learning at home

LE3027

ISBN 978-1-903670-96-5

© Alison Norman and Janette Smith

Illustrations © Bec Barnes

First published 2016

Printed in the UK for Lawrence Educational
PO Box 532, Cambridge, CB1 0BX, UK

Contents

Introduction

This book is designed to give early-years educators some starting points for developing children's interest in a mud kitchen. Mud is, after all, an ideal tactile learning medium, and it is inexpensive and easy to obtain. A mud kitchen can be a key element of outdoor continuous provision.

The activities in this book encourage the use of a mud kitchen throughout the year, and the guidance below should enable you to create such a kitchen.

Setting up a mud kitchen
- Involve everyone, including staff, children and their families, in planning and setting up your mud kitchen, which can be large or small scale, fixed or portable.
- Research and collect different designs of mud kitchens by using Google Images, Pinterest, Instagram, and so on.
- A portable mud kitchen can easily be set up in a builder's tray, while a more permanent one could be situated in a corner of your outdoor area or in an area sectioned off by low-level fencing.
- Old shelves, cupboards and pallets can be used to create your mud kitchen. Construct plenty of work surfaces – an old plank laid across two logs provides room to store pots, pans and woks.
- The children will need open access to materials such as soil, sand, gravel, plants, herbs, leaves, grasses, and so on.
- Provide a water source – an outside tap, water butt, hose pipe or water carrier.
- Make the kitchen and the materials you provide as natural and as open ended in their use as possible.
- Search charity shops and/or ask for donations from staff, families and friends to equip your mud kitchen with pots, pans, baking trays, kitchen utensils, washing-up bowls, and so on. Websites, such as www.freecycle.org, might also be useful.

Once the mud kitchen is in place and in use, this book will ensure that the area is being utilised to its full potential and that it is a place where high-quality learning occurs.

Mud is good for children! It connects them with nature and provides open-ended sensory experiences. Mud play activities, such as making mud pies, mixing ingredients, creating natural potions and perfumes are among some of the most memorable activities of childhood. Children who learn through mud-kitchen play have the opportunity to develop ideas and concepts and become creative thinkers. Children who have made soup, enjoyed a story or studied pictures of prehistoric art from around the world, for example, will have the knowledge and tools for their own investigative play in these and other areas.

The ideas in this book can be used flexibly to follow the needs and interests of the children. Every activity shows how a supportive adult can teach, model and respond to the children through their play. There are suggestions for ways to start conversations with children. However, the activities also include reminders that children sometimes need uninterrupted time to develop their own ideas and to play and explore.

How to use this book

This book has been written so that you can choose almost any activity and use it to spark children's interest and enhance their learning. Each page contains the following features:

- **Extra things to collect or make**: ideas for resources/equipment that might be in addition to your continuous provision and can enhance the activity. Most of these are inexpensive and easy to acquire, and many can be made with the children.
- **Setting the scene**: some starting points for developing children's interests in the mud kitchen. It includes ideas for how to involve children in planning and setting up activities and how adults can support high-quality learning experiences. Many sections provide guidance as to how activities can be extended to provide further challenge and learning opportunities.
- **What children might be learning**: highlights some of the main objectives for learning, while the open-ended nature of the activities means that children can learn at a level that is appropriate to their own development. All activities promote a cross-curricular approach to learning.
- **How children might be learning**: describes the positive learning behaviours that children might be using and developing through their play.
- **Book(s) and/or weblink(s)**: suggestions for fiction and non-fiction books, plus weblinks that will provide useful information.

Other considerations

Always include the children in agreeing ways to keep the mud kitchen a safe place to play in by:

- identifying and managing any risks and hazards, such as contamination of mud with animal faeces, trip and slip hazards and safety considerations when collecting flowers, leaves and berries.
- teaching the children to wash their hands after they have been playing in the mud kitchen, explaining to them the reasons why this is important.
- agreeing and developing routines for hand washing, the wearing of suitable clothing and ways of keeping the equipment clean, dry and rust free.

Mud is a great motivator. It is exciting and fun. We hope that you and your children enjoy these ideas!

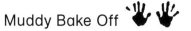

Starting with soup

Extra things to collect or make

* Ladles, large and small spoons
* Selection of recipe books
* Large cooking pots and pans
* Bowls of different sizes
* Natural containers, such as a hollowed-out pumpkin
* Kitchen timer.

Setting the scene

Read stories about making and eating delicious soup. Look at recipe books for inspiration, then make soup with the children and serve it as a snack or at lunchtime.

If you make pumpkin or squash soup in the autumn, you could scoop out the seeds and use them and the hollowed shell in the mud kitchen.

Encourage the children to make delicious mud soup! Support them in using language related to preparing and cooking soup, such as chopping, stirring, simmering and boiling.

* How long will the soup need to be cooked for?
* How many different ingredients are in the soup and what are they?
* What ingredients might you add to your soup to make it smell delicious?

Provide some chalk for a board painted with blackboard paint or pens for a large piece of paper/whiteboard. Encourage the children to draw or write their soup recipes.

What children might be learning

* to use cooking implements with safety and control as they make soup
* to use mathematical language when deciding which sized bowl to use and how long the soup needs to be cooked for.
* to use writing to record their soup recipes.

How children might be learning

* by testing out ideas and adding different ingredients
* by using mathematical ideas of size and time in their play in the mud kitchen
* by being supported by an adult to take their next steps when writing soup recipes.

Stone Soup by Jess Stockham (Child's Play, 2006)
Pumpkin Soup by Helen Cooper (Corgi Children's, 1999)

Soup recipes can be found at www.bbcgoodfood.com/howto/guide/best-soup-recipes-kids

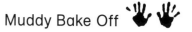

Seafood platter

Extra things to collect or make

* Selection of shells, especially flatter ones: scallop, oyster, cockle, limpet, mussel. (A local restauranteur or fishmonger might donate empty shells.)
* Range of cookery books
* Platters or large, clean scallop shells
* Smoked mackerel fillet, soft cheese, a lemon and slices of bread
* Toaster.

Setting the scene

Take the children to visit a fishmonger or the fish counter of your local supermarket. If you live close to the sea, it might be possible to visit a fishing harbour.

Talk with the children about whether they eat fish and/or shellfish and, if they do, what types they like or dislike. Look through the cookery books to find seafood recipes.

Make smoked mackerel pâté with the children by mixing a smoked mackerel fillet with soft cheese and a good squeeze of lemon juice. You could serve this on fingers of toast, using the large scallop shells as plates.

Use the shells in the mud kitchen. Support the children's thinking:

* Can you create seafood dishes by filling the shells with any ingredients you find outside?
* What fillings will you make?
* Can you use the shells as moulds?
* What names will you give your dishes?
* Can you make a large platter of stuffed shells?

* What patterns can you make in the mud using a shell?

What children might be learning

* to find out more about the shellfish people eat
* to read and enjoy an increasing range of books, including recipe books
* to create moulded shapes and patterns in the mud kitchen.

How children might be learning

* by using recipe books to find information about shellfish
* by being creative and experimenting with different shells and fillings
* by being pleased with the shapes and patterns they have made in the mud kitchen.

Mud Pies and Other Recipes by Marjorie Winslow and Erik Blegvad (New York Children's Collection, 2010)

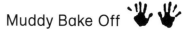

Spaghetti bolognaise and other favourites

Extra things to collect or make

* Range of cookery books
* Empty food cans that have smooth and safe edges
* Ingredients to put inside cans: pasta, stones, leaves, bark
* Cooking implements, cutlery and crockery
* Digital camera or other similar recording device.

Setting the scene

Share a collection of well-illustrated cookery books with the children.

Talk about favourite meals and encourage the children to think about meals eaten at different times, for example, on special days, in the summer, on cold days. Talk about who cooks at home or within their wider family.

Watch extracts from a cookery programme. See the weblink below.

Cook simple meals with the children.

Dip into *Mud Pies and Other Recipes*:

* What would you like to eat?
* What would you like to cook?
* Who would you cook for?

Encourage the children to make delicious and inventive mud dinners!

Support them in using language related to preparing and cooking food, such as chopping, stirring, boiling, roasting, grilling, frying.

Ask the children to take photographs of the meals they have created and use them to make a mud kitchen recipe book. Alternatively, record a short video clip of the children cooking, complete with their chef's voice-over!

What children might be learning

* to use technology to find out about meals and cooking and to make a mud kitchen recipe book or a Muddy Bake Off video
* to use the vocabulary of cooking as they make their mud dinners
* to understand that there is a sequence to preparing and cooking a meal.

How children might be learning

* by using technology to find and share information
* by talking aloud as they follow a sequence of actions in order to make their mud dinner
* by using the vocabulary of cooking that has been modelled to them by an adult.

Mud Pies and Other Recipes by Marjorie Winslow and Erik Blegvad (New York Children's Collection, 2010)

Episodes from the television series *Ready Steady Cook* can be found at www.bbc.co.uk/programmes/b006vcgr/episodes/guide

A muddy stir-fry

Extra things to collect or make

* Stir-fry ingredients: seasonal vegetables, rice or noodles
* Wok
* Knives, forks, spoons and chopsticks
* Bowls.

Setting the scene

Working together make a stir-fry using chopped seasonal vegetables from the local shop or your setting's garden. Stir fry them in a wok and serve with some cooked noodles or rice. Give the children a selection of cutlery, including some short chopsticks, and enjoy the food for a snack or lunch. Talk with the children about what they have eaten and what they eat at home:

* I wonder if you like the stir-fry.
* Do you like noodles or rice the best?
* Who eats with chopsticks at home?

Talk with the children about the importance of eating vegetables to help them to keep healthy and grow well.

Add a wok and chopsticks to the mud kitchen. Provide opportunities for the children to make and serve mud stir-fries, asking them what ingredients they will add to the wok. Encourage them to invent some stir-fry names. Join in to model language and ideas if the children need particular support.

Replenish or extend the resources as needed and allow the children plenty of time to develop their play.

What children might be learning

* to talk about food and how it is eaten in different parts of the world
* to use their imagination as they make muddy stir-fries
* to understand that it is a healthy choice to eat a variety of vegetables.

How children might be learning

* by being willing to try new foods and use new tools, such as chopsticks
* by being curious about similarities and differences in the foods people eat
* by knowing about some of the foods that contribute to a healthy diet.

The Runaway Wok by Ying Chang Compestine and Sebastia Serra (E.P. Dutton & Co, 2011)
The Story of Chopsticks by Ying Chang Compestine and Yongsheng Xuan (Holiday House, 2001)

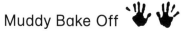

Flat breads, pancakes and chapatis

Extra things to collect or make

✷ Chapatis and a range of fillings
✷ Large map of the world
✷ Sticky mud or clay
✷ Large leaves from your local setting.

Setting the scene

Read *Mama Panya's Pancakes*. Talk about the kinds of pancake or flat bread the children have eaten before. The book gives several examples of flat cakes from around the world:

- blinis from Russia
- bannocks from Scotland
- crêpes from France
- chapatis from India
- bao bing from China
- tortillas from Mexico.

Make some chapatis or buy some ready-made ones and let the children fill them with sweet or savoury fillings, before rolling or folding them and tucking in. Alternatively, make large pancakes and add lemon and sugar, before rolling or folding them.

Use the large map to mark some other places in the world where particular pancakes and flat breads originate from.

Add sticky mud or clay to the mud kitchen and invite the children to make muddy pancakes and flat breads, asking:

- How flat and round can you make your muddy pancake?
- Can you use a large leaf filled with mud as your flat bread or chapati?

- What can you use to serve your pancake with?
- What fillings might you want to collect to add your pancake?

The children might want to make an outdoor pretend fire like the real one in *Mama Panya's Pancakes* for some of their cooking.

What children might be learning

✷ to talk about food and how it is eaten in different parts of the world
✷ to use a map to find different countries
✷ to use fine motor skills to roll and fold flat breads, pancakes and chapatis.

How children might be learning

✷ by being sensitive to other cultures and traditions when making flat breads, pancakes and chapatis
✷ by asking questions to find out about what people in other countries like to eat
✷ by being motivated and wanting to extend their play in the mud kitchen.

Mama Panya's Pancakes by Mary Chamberlin, Richard Chamberlin and Julia Cairns (Barefoot Books, 2006)

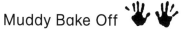

Pizza delivery

Extra things to collect or make

* Cardboard pizza boxes (many companies will donate some if asked)
* Pizza restaurant resources: telephones, a till and money, order pads and clipboards, pencils, pizza menus
* Delivery bikes and other vehicles.

Setting the scene

Talk with the children about eating pizza, asking:

- Who has eaten pizza?
- Who has eaten it at home?
- Who has been to a pizza restaurant?
- Who has had pizza delivered to their home?
- What toppings do you like the best?

If you have a pizza delivery service in your area, you could order pizza for a snack. Discuss the following questions over the snack:

- What information did the restaurant need to know?
- How did the driver know where to come?
- How does the driver keep the pizza warm?

Make your own pizzas and give the children the opportunity to choose from a range of toppings.

Plan with the children how to turn the mud kitchen into a pizza restaurant and delivery service, asking:

- What will you need to make and cook mud pizzas?
- What will be on the menu and what will it look like?
- What toppings will be available?

Provide opportunities for children to write down orders, take names, addresses and telephone numbers. Join in with the play and model language and ideas if the children need extra support.

Replenish or extend the resources as needed and allow the children plenty of time to develop their play.

What children might be learning

* to talk about familiar experiences and appreciate that pizzas can be delivered, bought at a shop or made at home
* to use numbers in their play as they phone the pizza delivery company and pay for the mud pizzas
* to write for a purpose as they create menus and take orders.

How children might be learning

* by suggesting ideas to create a muddy pizza restaurant and working with others to make it successful
* by developing their ideas and being interested in adding more details to the pizza restaurant
* by becoming fascinated by numbers in everyday life.

Pizza at Sally's by Monica Wellington (Dutton Books, 2006)

A simple pizza recipe can be found at www.bbc.co.uk/cbeebies/makes/i-can-cook-easypeasypizza

Muddy kebabs

Extra things to collect or make

* Wooden kebab sticks
* Food for kebabs
* Clay or sticky mud
* Sticks from the garden
* Grill racks
* Long platters
* Role-play campfire.

Setting the scene

Make fruit kebabs with the children using cooking-grade wooden kebab sticks. Offer a selection of fruit or savoury ingredients and ask the children to choose from them for their kebab. If you have access to a fire pit, you could help the children to cook a wider range of foods on appropriate skewers.

Eat the kebabs that have been made and talk about the different ingredients and flavours used. Talk about how important eating plenty of fruit and vegetables is for good health.

Add sticks and sticky mud to the mud kitchen, as well as some grill racks and long platters. Send the children off to collect items to put onto sticks to make muddy kebabs. This is a good opportunity to encourage the children to make a pattern of ingredients on their sticks.

Provide opportunities for children to make, cook and serve mud kebabs, using the role-play campfire. Join in with their play and model language and ideas if the children need additional support.

What children might be learning

* to use their imagination as they make muddy kebabs
* to choose a good variety of fruit and vegetables, which can contribute to a healthy lifestyle
* to use different items to create patterns on their kebab sticks.

How children might be learning

* by showing through actions and language what they know about healthy eating
* by knowing about some of the foods that contribute to a healthy diet
* by paying attention to detail while making patterns on kebab sticks.

Children's Step-by-Step Cookbook by Angela Wilkes (Dorling Kindersley, 2003)

Kebab recipes can be found at www.bbcgoodfood.com/recipes/rainbow-fruit-skewers

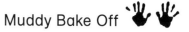

Ice cream for pudding!

Extra things to collect or make

* Thick Greek yoghurt
* Chopped fruit / fruit puree
* Small freezer tubs / ice-lolly moulds
* Ice-cream scoops
* Squeezy bottles
* Plastic sundae dishes and small spoons
* Toppings: glitter, dried herbs, small sticks, clean lollipop sticks, shells
* Damp sand.

Setting the scene

Make ice cream using Greek yoghurt and chopped fruit / fruit puree with the children. Freeze the mixtures in small tubs or in ice-lolly moulds with sticks. While enjoying the ice-cream together, talk with the children about their favourite ice-cream flavours. You might also explore:

* Who likes to add sprinkles or sauce to their ice cream?
* When and where have you had ice cream?
* Have you bought ice cream from an ice-cream van?

Plan with the children how to turn the mud kitchen into an ice-cream van or shop, asking:

* What will you need to make mud ice cream?
* What equipment might be useful?
* What flavours of ice cream will be on sale?
* What toppings and sauces will be available?

Provide opportunities for the children to invent and make mud ice creams. Ask them to draw and label a poster showing the different ice creams that are available. Encourage them to invent some ice-cream names.

Join in with the play and model language and ideas if the children need additional support.

Replenish or extend the resources as needed and allow the children plenty of time to develop their play.

What children might be learning

* to observe and investigate freezing and melting
* to talk about likes and dislikes and understand that other children do not always enjoy the same things as they do
* to use pictures and writing to advertise the ice creams they have made.

How children might be learning

* by exploring what happens when they make real ice cream
* by using their experiences to recreate and make ice cream in the mud kitchen
* by working with other children and adults to advertise their ice creams.

Ice Cream Summer by Peter Sis (Scholastic Press, 2015)

Frozen dessert recipes can be found at
www.bbcgoodfood.com/howto/guide/our-best-ever-ice-lolly-recipes

Muddy milkshakes

Extra things to collect or make

* Whisks, spoons and jugs
* Cornflour and water
* Food colouring or crushed coloured chalk
* Plastic milk cartons
* Clear plastic glasses.

Setting the scene

Make milkshakes with the children and find out what they know about them:

* Do you drink milkshakes at home?
* Do you have them as a treat when you go out?
* What flavours do you prefer?

Talk about the health benefits of drinking milk, but explain that most milkshakes also contain a lot of sugar, so drinking too many can be unhealthy.

Plan with the children how to turn the mud kitchen into a milkshake bar:

* What will you need to make mud milkshakes?
* Where will you make the drinks?
* Where will people sit to drink their milkshakes?
* What flavours will be on sale?

Make some 'milk' using water and cornflour. Decant the mixture into the cartons and put them in the mud-kitchen fridge. Provide opportunities for children to invent and make mud milkshakes, asking the following:

* What happens when you whisk up the muddy milkshakes?
* Can you make different coloured milkshakes?

Ask them to draw and label a poster showing the different milkshakes that are available. Encourage them to invent some names for their drinks.

What children might be learning

* to observe how materials change when they are mixed together
* to express themselves effectively and be aware of their audience when talking about milkshakes
* to use pictures and writing to make posters about the milkshakes they have made.

How children might be learning

* by testing out ideas and adding different ingredients to their milkshakes
* by thinking of ideas and sharing them effectively with others
* by working with other children and adults to make the muddy-milkshake posters.

Children's Step-by-Step Cookbook by Angela Wilkes (Dorling Kindersley, 2003)

Milkshake recipes can be found at
www.buzzle.com/articles/how-to-make-healthy-milkshakes-for-kids.html

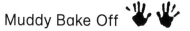

A mud picnic

Extra things to collect or make

* Selection of lunch boxes and bags
* Waxed paper, large leaves
* Washable picnic blankets
* Equipment for an outdoor adventure: backpacks, maps, compasses, clipboards, pens.

Setting the scene

Plan an outdoor picnic with the children.

* Where shall we go?
* What shall we take?
* What types of food are best for a picnic?
* Will it be a snack-time, lunchtime or teatime picnic?

Prepare the food together, pack it up and set out on your adventure, even if it is only to the far side of your outdoor area! Take a suitable book, such as one of those listed here, to read after your feast.

Back in the mud kitchen, encourage the children to make picnic food and create their own picnic feasts.

* How many people are going on the picnic?
* How much food will you need?
* What types of food are easy to carry and eat with your fingers?
* Can you wrap your sandwiches, samosas and other food in leaves or paper?

Encourage the children to set up the picnic blankets away from the mud kitchen – every picnic should involve some travel and adventure! Maps, both printed and home made, and compasses will help the children to develop their imaginative play. Support the children as they follow and explore their own interests: a fairy picnic, a pirate picnic, or, perhaps even, a Jurassic picnic!

What children might be learning

* to plan and prepare a picnic, understanding that others might make different food choices to theirs
* to make and read maps to help them find their way to their picnic spot
* to use their imagination as they make fantasy picnics in the mud kitchen.

How children might be learning

* by sharing stories about picnics and using the ideas in their play
* by using maps to talk about places, directions and features of the environment
* by being supported by an adult to follow their own interests as they develop different ideas for going on a picnic.

A Picnic with Monet by Julie Merberg and Suzanne Bober (Chronicle Books, 2003)
Picnic by John Burningham (Red Fox, 2014)
Ants at the Picnic by Michael Dahl and Zachary Trover (Picture Windows Books, 2006)

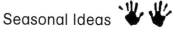

Muddy puddles

Extra things to collect or make

☀ Wet-weather clothing and boots
☀ Big sticks for stirring
☀ Metre sticks and lengths of string.

Setting the scene

It is raining hard again! Talk with the children about what they will need to wear when they go outside. Perhaps you have a teddy bear who sits by the door wearing the correct clothing for the weather.

Encourage the children to explore all the puddles they can find:

- Can you jump in a puddle?
- Can you leap across a puddle?
- Can you run around a puddle?
- Can you wade through a puddle?
- What happens if you stir the water in a puddle?
- What ingredients from the mud kitchen will you add to a puddle?
- Whose puddle is the biggest?
- Whose puddle is the deepest?
- How can you find out?

Let the children measure their chosen puddle with their feet / stride / length of string / metre stick.

Leave the pots, pans and woks from the mud kitchen out to collect any rainwater that falls overnight so that the children can make their own puddles.

What children might be learning

☀ to use positional language as they explore puddles
☀ to use non-standard and standard measures to compare the size of puddles
☀ to keep warm, dry and safe when playing outside in the rain.

How children might be learning

☀ by understanding that they need to keep themselves and others safe when jumping in puddles
☀ by thinking of different ways to solve the problem of measuring puddles
☀ by working in a small team to measure puddles.

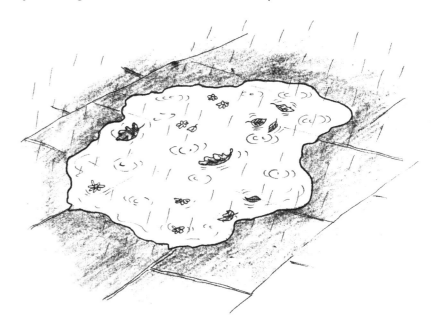

One Duck Stuck by Phyllis Root and Jane Chapman (Walker Books, 1999)

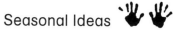

Pumpkin soup

Extra things to collect or make

* Pumpkins and squashes of differing sizes
* Cauldron-sized bowls
* Big sticks for stirring soup
* Leaves, moss, sticks, pebbles.

Setting the scene

Ideally, you will have grown pumpkins from seed with the children. However, if this has not been possible, look at and talk about pictures of pumpkins growing in a field.

Collect different types, sizes and colours of pumpkins and squashes, allowing the children to explore them using their senses. Extend children's vocabulary by using descriptive language, such as smooth, bumpy, tall, short, slippery, soft, hard, heavy, light.

Make some pumpkin soup with the children and eat it together at snack time.

Help the children to remove the tops of the pumpkins in the mud kitchen. Look together at the amazing stringy, wet pulp inside the hollow-sounding pumpkin. Help the children to remove the pulp by hand. Discuss the following:

* I wonder if we could make some pumpkin pie or soup with this.
* What might we add to the pumpkin to make it tastier?
* How should we cook it?
* Will it take long to cook?

Encourage the children to use the pumpkin pulp and flesh in the mud kitchen to create new dishes, adding ingredients of their own choosing, such as leaves, moss, sticks and pebbles.

Write down the children's recipes and produce a pumpkin recipe book for the mud kitchen.

What children might be learning

* to talk about the sensory experiences they feel when exploring pumpkins and squashes
* to talk about how plants grow from seeds and that pumpkins and squashes contain such seeds
* to cook pumpkins and squashes and talk about what they have done.

How children might be learning

* by being willing to use all their senses to explore pumpkins
* by putting their observations into words and talking about what they can see and feel
* by making connections between the different things they have seen and learned about pumpkins.

Pumpkin Soup by Helen Cooper (Corgi Children's Books, 1999)
Seed, Sprout, Pumpkin, Pie by Jill Esbaum (National Geographic Kids, 2009)

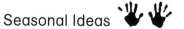

A snow kitchen

Extra things to collect or make

* Buckets, brooms, snow scoops
* Resources to sprinkle on snow: glitter, coloured sand, salt, sugar, flour, bird seed
* Jelly moulds, silicone cake cases, ice-cube trays, ice-cream tubs
* Food colouring
* Warm and cold water
* Washing-up liquid.

Setting the scene

What excitement! It has snowed overnight and the children are eager to go outside and play. Provide buckets, brooms and snow scoops to enable the children to move the snow around. Encourage the children to draw in the snow using sticks, make footprints in the snow, roll snowballs and build snowmen.

The mud kitchen has become a snow kitchen! Collect twigs and leaves to use in the snow kitchen. Let the children experiment with the different materials provided, supporting their ideas and thinking:

* Can you make some snow cakes by hand or using a mould?
* How might you decorate your cakes?
* What might happen if you add some salt to snow?
* What might happen if we leave some water in the ice-cube trays overnight?
* What happened when we tried to make a cup of tea with the snow?
* What happens when you pour warm water onto snow?

Allow the children to leave their cakes in the mud kitchen ready for the next day. What might happen to the cakes during the night?

What children might be learning

* to appreciate that snow can be shaped and moulded and can be changed by adding different materials to it
* to understand that water freezes when it is very cold and that snow and ice melt as the temperature increases
* to describe how they experimented with snow and ice, what they observed and what they found out.

How children might be learning

* by making links between the temperature, what they did and what happened to the snow and ice
* by thinking of ways to stop the snow and ice melting
* by talking with other children and adults about what they did and what worked well.

Elmer in the Snow by David McKee (Andersen Press, 2008)
Kipper's Snowy Day by Mick Inkpen (Hodder Children's Books, 2015)

Christmas in the mud kitchen

Extra things to collect or make

* Cake ingredients: acorns, pine cones, conkers, bark pieces, pieces of citrus peel
* Pudding basins, bun and cake tins
* Christmas plates and dishes
* Silver sand and glitter in spice shakers
* Cake decorations and tinsel
* Digital camera or similar device
* Empty mince-pie boxes and foil cases.

Setting the scene

Time to start cooking for Christmas! Talk with the children about what special treats they enjoy at this time of year:

* Who likes chocolate log / mince pies / Christmas pudding / Christmas cake?
* What other food is important to you?
* What other food do you have at special celebrations?

Use food magazines and/or recipe websites with the children to collect pictures of seasonal food.

Now get baking! Prompt the play by asking:

* What are you going to bake today?
* What ingredients are you going to use?
* How long will it take to cook?
* How might you decorate it when it is cooked?

Extend the children's vocabulary by using descriptive language, such as mix, stir, add, sprinkle, decorate, bake, ingredients.

Invite the children to take photographs of their cakes and puddings to make a Christmas recipe book for the mud kitchen.

What children might be learning

* to recognise and/or describe special times for themselves and their family
* to find relevant sources of information, including in books, magazines and the Internet
* to select materials and mix them together to make different textures.

How children might be learning

* by making predictions about what might happen when they mix different materials together to make Christmas food
* by exploring ideas about Christmas food in open-ended play
* by responding to an adult challenge to record their Christmas recipes by taking photographs.

Christmas Cooking for Children (Usborne Books, 2009)

Christmas recipe books or magazines
Christmas recipes can be found by searching www.bbcgoodfood.com

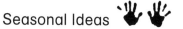

Valentine's Day chocolates

Extra things to collect or make

* Empty chocolate boxes with their plastic trays and booklets
* Chocolate and some means to melt it, along with fruit to dip in it
* Silver foil and coloured cellophane pieces
* A variety of toppings: beads, buttons, petals, seeds, small pebbles.

Setting the scene

At this time of year the shops are full of boxes of chocolates!

Children will understand more about making chocolates if they have helped to melt chocolate, dipping fruit into it as a tasty treat or using it to make simple cakes.

Share a book about chocolate with the children.

Help the children to turn the mud kitchen into a chocolate factory by having conversations such as:

* Where will the chocolate be heated to make it melt?
* What will be mixed into it?
* How can it be shaped and moulded?
* How will you make the chocolates look delicious?
* How many chocolates are there in each tray?
* How many people will be sharing these chocolates?
* How many have you made of each kind?

Look at the pictures and names on a chocolate box and ask the children to invent some fabulous names for their mud chocolates. Which kind of chocolate would each child like the best?

Now you have made all those delicious chocolates, look at the next page and make a mud kitchen chocolate shop.

What children might be learning

* to use language to describe chocolate – melted, runny, hard, sticky, decorated, shaped – and employ these words and others to describe their creations
* to develop mathematical ideas, including more and less, full and empty, number names and one-to-one correspondence to count objects, and words to describe 3-D shapes
* to ask questions and think about where chocolate comes from and how it is made.

How children might be learning

* by using what they already know about chocolates to help them to plan and create a chocolate factory
* by using resources in imaginative ways to invent, make and name amazing mud chocolates
* by talking about what they like and dislike and discovering what other people like best.

But I Do Know All About Chocolate by Lauren Child (Puffin Books, 2007)

The chocolate shop

Extra things to collect or make

* A till and 1p coins
* Bags and boxes for the mud chocolates
* Materials to create price lists, labels and posters.

Setting the scene

Now that you have a mud kitchen full of chocolates, help the children to plan and set up a chocolate shop.

Visit a local chocolate shop or find some photographs of a chocolate shop on the Internet. Plan how the mud kitchen chocolate shop will look, with prompts such as:

* How will you ask for what you need?
* How will you get the chocolates ready to sell?
* How many chocolates can you fit into each box?
* How much will they cost?
* How are you going to display your chocolates?
* Who will work in the shop and who will visit it?
* What will you say to your customers?

Support the children as they make price lists, labels, bags and posters. Invent delicious-sounding names for the chocolates!

Invite parents and carers to the mud kitchen chocolate shop.

What children might be learning

* to explore the role of customer and shop assistant, such as asking questions and responding to requests
* to apply different ways of calculating the money needed to pay for some chocolates
* to design, make and write information on labels, posters and bags.

How children might be learning

* by using what they already know about shopping to help them to plan and create a chocolate shop
* by acting out scenarios with other children and adults, and taking different roles in the shop
* by demonstrating their knowledge of money and counting in their play.

But I Do Know All About Chocolate by Lauren Child (Puffin Books, 2007)

Spring nests

Extra things to collect or make

* Straw, sticks, moss, feathers
* Bird puppets
* Clay (for making eggs)
* Pictures of birds' nests or an old nest
* Simple and unused bird boxes.

Setting the scene

Take the children outside to look and listen for signs of spring, paying special attention to any birds that are seen or heard.

If you have any bird puppets, hide them in the outdoor environment for the children to find. Share books and pictures about garden birds, encouraging the children to use this knowledge to help them to identify the birds they see, using the correct bird names.

Talk with the children about what they know about birds and what they would like to find out. Talk together about why the children are hearing and seeing more birds in spring compared to winter.

Look at pictures of birds' nests or an old nest, if you have one. Encourage the children to talk about what they might need to collect to make a bird's nest. Ask the children to make nests for the bird puppets, exploring:

* What kind of nest will you make?
* How will it fit together?
* How will you make sure it is big enough?
* Will you need to leave your nest to dry before testing it?

• How many eggs has your bird laid in the nest?

What children might be learning

* to observe and talk about birds in the spring
* to recognise and appreciate that the environment changes according to the season
* to use non-fiction books to find out information.

How children might be learning

* by being curious about how birds behave
* by becoming fascinated about the world around them and by springtime changes
* by exploring ideas, such as how birds' nests are made, and talking about the challenges the children faced when making their nests.

RSPB First Book of Birds by Anita Ganeri, David Chandler and Mike Unwin (A&C Black, 2011)

In the garden

Extra things to collect or make

* Seeds, including beans and peas
* Seed packets and labels
* Seedlings, such as bedding plants in trays
* Plant pots of different sizes, seed trays, potting trays
* Compost
* Gardening equipment: trowels, forks, watering cans, gardening gloves
* Photographs and pictures of gardens.

Setting the scene

Look together at the photographs and pictures of gardens. Talk with the children about the gardens they know or visit a garden or an allotment.

Plant beans, peas or other seeds with the children and watch them grow. Ask the children to take photographs of the plants as they grow and use them to make a class record.

Look through seed catalogues and magazines, exploring the following:

* What kinds of plant would you like to grow?
* Would you prefer a flower garden or a fruit and vegetable plot?
* What will you need to plant your seeds?
* What will your plants need to help them to grow?

Allow the children to play with seeds, plants, soil and other resources. Observe how they play and help them to explore their ideas and interests. Follow their lead and think about things together.

Model and encourage the correct vocabulary, such as leaves, roots, stem, seeds, petals, soil and compost.

Challenge the children to write labels for their plants, make seed packets and/or flower catalogues.

What children might be learning

* to use the correct words to talk about plants and growing
* to be aware of how things grow and change
* to write labels for their plants and/or to make seed packets.

How children might be learning

* by exploring what happens when they plant seeds and watch them grow
* by continuing to be interested in how things grow
* by thinking about what might happen and what they need to do, such as give their plants water, light, and so on.

Titch by Pat Hutchins (Red Fox, 1997)

Seed catalogues and gardening magazines

Making perfume

Extra things to collect or make

* Small piece of sponge for each child
* Small bottle containing coloured water
* Perfume ingredients: fresh herbs, flowers, petals, leaves, coloured water, glitter
* Smooth stones and small plastic bowls or pestle and mortar
* Perfume preparation tools: small plastic bottles, funnels, plastic droppers and sieves
* Writing materials for perfume recipes, including labels.

Setting the scene

Go for a walk outside and give each child a small piece of sponge dipped in 'special' coloured water. Explain that this will help them to smell what is all around them. Encourage them to rub their sponge gently on different surfaces, lean in close and smell what they have rubbed.

Stock the mud kitchen with the perfume ingredients above. Encourage the children to use them to mix their own perfumes. If you allow the children to collect their own ingredients, make sure you agree on clear rules about what can/cannot be picked/ gathered and used.

Extend the children's vocabulary by using descriptive language related to the process of perfume making, such as crushing, mixing, straining, dropping, pouring, smelling.

Encourage the children's thinking by asking:

* What did you use to make your perfume?
* Can you write your perfume recipe down so that someone else could make it?
* What does your perfume smell like?
* What is the name of your perfume?

What children might be learning

* to use descriptive language to talk about natural perfumes
* to explore how some materials change when they are crushed and added to water
* to write recipes and labels for their perfumes.

How children might be learning

* by being curious about the natural world, especially through the sense of smell
* by having their own ideas and testing them out to make different perfumes
* by being creative through their writing.

Mo Smells Green by Margaret Hyde (Mo's Nose, 2009)

Dry summer mud

Extra things to collect or make

* Colanders and sieves
* Empty spice shakers
* Funnels and spoons
* Dry sand
* Weighing scales.

Setting the scene

Summer has arrived at last and the mud pies keep drying out!

Talk with the children about what they think might happen if no more water is available in the mud kitchen. Encourage the children to identify some sunny spots in the outdoor area that might be good for cooking mud pies. Leave moulded mud and trays of mud in the sunny spots. Support the children by asking:

* Which mud dried out first and why?
* What happened to the moulded mud?
* How does dry mud look and feel?
* How is it different from wet mud?

Add sand to the mud kitchen and explore how wet and dry sand are different from mud.

Once you have enough dry mud and sand, add colanders, sieves and spice shakers to the mud kitchen. Explore what comes through the holes and what does not.

Experiment with what can be made with dry mud.

If it has not rained, reintroduce the water supply and encourage the children to experience the joy of turning dry soil and sand into heavy, sticky mud!

What children might be learning

* to understand that wet mud can be shaped and moulded, but dry mud crumbles and loses its moulded shape more easily
* to understand that mud dries out when it is left in the sun
* to talk about the differences between wet and dry mud.

How children might be learning

* by noticing and wondering why wet mud changes into dry mud when it is left in the sun
* by sustaining interest over a few days as the mud dries out
* by suggesting ideas for what to do with the dry mud.

Mud by Mary Lyn Ray and Lauren Stringer (Harcourt Brace International, 2001)

Muddy painting

Extra things to collect or make

✳ Mark-making implements: DIY paintbrushes, sticks, small sponges

✳ Large painting surfaces: clean paving, thick paper, cardboard, fabric

✳ Colouring materials: powder paint, food colouring

✳ Coloured chalks

✳ Pestle and mortar.

Setting the scene

Help the children to make the mud kitchen into an art workshop, providing large painting surfaces.

Encourage the children to experiment with making marks using mud.

- What kind of marks and patterns can you make with mud paint and brushes/hands/fingers?
- What happens if you add something to make coloured mud paint?
- What happens if you add more water to the paint?

Once the children have explored making and using mud paints, introduce information and ideas about ancient cave art, which was created using paint made from pigments from rocks and soils.

This is a good opportunity to use the Internet to look for images of cave paintings and rock art from around the world and find their locations on a map. The following are some fabulous examples to begin with:

- Lascaux: France (www.lascaux.culture.fr/?lng=en#/fr/00.xml for a virtual tour)

- Pech Merle: France (www.pechmerle.com/english/index.php for a virtual tour)
- Laas Geel: Somaliland
- Kakadu: Australia
- Altamira: Spain
- Cueva de la Manos: Argentina
- Nine Mile Canyon: United States of America
- Magura: Bulgaria.

Continue to encourage the children to make mud paints and create their own paintings and patterns.

What children might be learning

✳ to use the Internet to find out about cave paintings around the world

✳ to use reference material such as maps, an atlas or a globe to find different places

✳ to experiment with mud, water and colour to create imaginative designs.

How children might be learning

✳ by understanding that the art they create is part of a long tradition of painting with mud and coloured soils

✳ by experimenting with a range of materials and tools to make artwork

✳ by locating places around the world on a map, atlas or globe and talking about what can be seen there.

Cave Baby by Julia Donaldson and Emily Gravett (Macmillan Children's Books, 2011)

The Internet is a rich source of images of cave paintings from around the world

Muddy drips and drops

Extra things to collect or make

* A collection of tools for sucking up water and making drips and drops: turkey basters, empty squeezy bottles, Twisty droppers (available from Yellow Door)
* Small watering cans with rose attachments
* Fairly dry soil in bowls or trays, plus extra water.

Setting the scene

Set out the new resources so that the children can experiment with them in the mud kitchen.

Encourage the children to add water to the soil little by little in drips and drops. You might need to model how to do this if the tools are completely new to the children, along with how to wait and watch to see what happens as the water falls onto the soil.

- What happens when drops of water first hit the soil?
- What happens to the water?
- What happens to the soil?

Sooner or later the dry soil will transform into mud! Encourage the children to carry on exploring, asking:

- Can you make muddy drops?
- What happens if you try to suck up thick mud?
- What happens if the mud is thin?
- What comes out of the droppers and what stays inside?

Eventually you will need to clean out all those muddy basters and droppers in the water tray. This is almost as much fun as it was getting them muddy in the first place!

What children might be learning

* to use one-handed tools, such as basters and droppers
* to use simple tools to add water to soil and then to observe any changes
* to explain what they are doing and describe what they can see happening.

How children might be learning

* by exploring new resources and persevering until they are expert in using them
* by becoming competent in using tools and materials to make muddy drips and drops
* by making links and noticing patterns when investigating drips and drops.

Water Can Be… by Laura Purdie Salas and Violeta Dabija (Millbrook Press, 2014)

Making moulds

Extra things to collect or make

* Range of moulds: jelly, cake, chocolate, ice-cube
* Large bowls
* Large sandwich platters
* Decorative materials: buttons, beads, leaves, dried flowers, shells.

Setting the scene

Introduce the different moulds into classroom activities, including cooking, using wet sand and play dough and water play. Encourage the children to talk about what happens when they put different materials into moulds and turn them out.

Have a 'mouldy day' in the mud kitchen, which could lead on to other conversations!

Use large bowls to mix mud and water together. Allow the children to test whether the consistency is right for turning out a perfect shape from a mould.

* What happens when you turn out your mould?
* Was your mud too sticky, too crumbly, too thick or just right?
* How can you make your mud mixture better?

Let the children display their moulded shapes on the sandwich platters.

Encourage further explorations, by asking:

* What can you find to decorate your moulded shapes with?
* Can you find anything else nearby that will make a good mould?

What children might be learning

* to experiment in order to find out how well different materials, such as sand, mud and dough, make moulded shapes
* to use extended vocabulary, such as sticky, crumbly and gritty, to describe the different properties of materials
* to develop their creativity by choosing how to decorate their shapes.

How children might be learning

* by testing out different ideas and evaluating what works well when using moulds
* by enjoying learning new vocabulary and being proud when they use new words to describe the moulded shapes
* by persisting with their mould making and decoration, even when challenges occur.

Jellies and Their Moulds by Peter Brears (Prospect Books, 2010)

Bricks and muddy mortar

Extra things to collect or make

* Building materials: bricks, wooden planks, soil, sand
* Tools for mixing and spreading: spades, trowels, buckets, wheelbarrows
* Builder's toolkit: tape measure, small spirit level, ruler, clipboard, pencil, plans and pictures of buildings
* Noticeboard.

Setting the scene

Walk past a building site with the children, share a book on building a house (see below) or view online images of bricklaying and building.

Introduce the vocabulary the children will need, including words such as cement, mortar, trowel, layer and smooth.

Provide the resources for the children to create a building site next to the mud kitchen. Talk with the children about how to stay safe when lifting, moving and fixing bricks. Discuss why it is a good idea to build a long, low structure rather than a tall tower.

Encourage the children to work together to plan and to build.

* What pattern of bricks makes the strongest structure?
* What mix of soil, sand and water makes good cement?
* How long is your wall?
* How can you tell if it is straight?

Provide a noticeboard next to the building site. Encourage the children to display safety notices, rules, resource lists, plans and photographs.

What children might be learning

* to use bricklaying and building tools competently and appropriately
* to explore ideas about buildings and constructions
* to build and create using mathematical concepts, including shape and pattern.

How children might be learning

* by predicting what might happen when they mix different materials to make cement
* by being confident to try out their own ideas when building a structure
* by recording and sharing their accomplishments using photographs and drawings.

Building a House by Byron Barton (Turtleback Books, 1999)

Mud sculptures

Extra things to collect or make

* Quick-drying clay
* Dried flowers
* Sticks and leaves
* Pine cones
* Pictures of sculptures.

Setting the scene

Allow the children to explore the quick-drying clay, asking:

* What does it feel like?
* Can you mould the clay into different shapes?
* What happens when you add a little water to the clay?

Share pictures and photographs of sculptures. You might want to focus on a particular theme, such as people, animals or abstract.

Give the children an opportunity to create their own sculpture by shaping their piece of clay.

Provide children with materials to decorate their sculptures, as well as encouraging them to explore the outdoor area and collect anything else they might want to use. For instance, they might want to make a hedgehog and need small twigs for its spikes.

Change your mud kitchen into an exhibition space and encourage the children to display their art work. Some children might want to write a brief description to explain their work to others.

Take photographs of the children's work and use the printed versions to make 'Our Book of Sculptures' for your book area.

What children might be learning

* to be interested in and describe the texture of clay
* to plan their sculpture and mould their clay to achieve their design
* to create an exhibition area using photographs, sculptures and written explanations.

How children might be learning

* by planning and making decisions about how they will make an exhibition area to show their sculptures
* by being proud of their finished sculptures
* by being able to talk about what they are about to do, what they are doing, what worked well and what they might change next time.

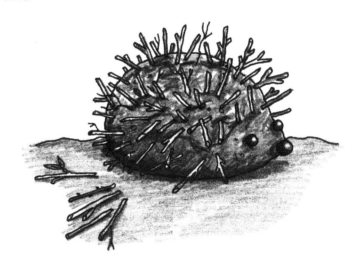

13 Sculptures Children Should Know by Angela Wenzel (Prestel, 2010)

'Our Book of Sculptures' as created by the children in your setting

Mud pomanders

Extra things to collect or make

* Cloves
* Satsumas/oranges
* Clay
* String
* Sticks
* Herb garden or herb plants
* Aromatics: flowers, lavender, items from herb garden.

Setting the scene

Show the children pictures of pomanders and talk about why people living long ago wanted to carry something sweet-smelling with them. Children will love to think about all the horrible smells that would have been part of daily life in the past! Read *The Smelly Book* and talk about smells that the children do not like and smells that make them think about nicer things.

Use little easy-peel satsumas or similar and cloves to make simple pomanders with the children. Instructions can be found on the Herb Society's schools' website, using the address given below.

The pomanders will keep well if they are dried in a warm environment.

Encourage the children to make pomanders in the mud kitchen.

* Can you make a ball of mud and clay?
* Can you attach your clay ball to a piece of string or a stick?
* What will you add to your clay ball to make it into a pomander that smells good?

Encourage the children to use their sense of smell to choose materials to press into their pomander:

* Which of these herbs and flowers have a smell that you like?
* Think about how the pomander will look. Can you make shapes or patterns on the ball with what you've chosen?

What children might be learning

* to talk about smells that they like or dislike and listen to children who might have different views
* to discuss how people lived in the past
* to develop fine-motor skills by making a clay ball, fixing it to a piece of string or a stick and adding other items.

How children might be learning

* by using their senses to help them to choose materials to make a pomander
* by persevering while making their pomanders
* by talking about problems they encounter while making their pomander and suggesting ways in which they can solve the them.

The Smelly Book by Babette Cole (Red Fox, 2001)

Pictures of pomanders from the Internet: www.herbsociety.org.uk/schools/activities/pomander.htm

Sunken treasure

Extra things to collect or make

* Seabed materials: stones, gravel, sand
* Treasure: stones sprayed gold, glass nuggets, shiny buttons, old jewels, chains
* Props for pirates: hats, eye patches, bandanas, wide belts
* Treasure-seeking tools: net bags, strainers, small fishing nets, sticks, string
* Old sink or tray full of mud or sand, deep enough for burying treasure.

Setting the scene

Fire the imagination of the children with tales of sunken galleons and buried treasure, extending their vocabulary by using words related to pirate ships and treasure. Encourage the children to invent stories about pirate adventures.

* I wonder why a ship full of treasure might end up at the bottom of the ocean.
* Who might be searching for it?
* What might they do with the treasure if they find it?

Make a thick layer of stones, gravel or sand at the bottom of the sink/tray. Add some water and stir in some mud so that the water becomes mysteriously murky. Now sink the treasure into the depths.

* What might be at the bottom of the mud-kitchen ocean?
* How might you search for any buried treasure?

Explore the treasure you find.

* How many pieces of gold have you found?

* How many jewels?
* Who has the most/least treasure?

What children might be learning

* to invent characters, settings and events for their pirate stories
* to use language and story structure in their sunken treasure play that reflects the stories that they have heard and read
* to count treasure and compare how many different objects they have found.

How children might be learning

* by using ideas that they know about pirates and treasure in their stories and role play
* by feeling confident enough to contribute their ideas to the stories about pirates
* by playing co-operatively and taking turns with others.

Pirates Love Underpants by Claire Freedman and Ben Cort (Simon & Schuster, 2013)

Buried treasure

Extra things to collect or make

✳ Treasure: stones sprayed gold, glass nuggets, shiny buttons, old jewels, chains

✳ Treasure-hunting props: maps, small spades, trowels, paper and felt pens

✳ Mud-kitchen sink or trays full of mud or sand, deep enough to bury treasure in.

Setting the scene

If this is your first pirate adventure in the mud kitchen, set the scene with stories and poems, providing opportunities for role play and small-world play beforehand.

If you have used the ideas from Sunken treasure (page 31), explain to the children that now they have rescued the treasure from the bottom of the mud ocean, it is time to be a good pirate and bury it somewhere safe!

Encourage the children to make treasure islands in the sink or mud trays.

- What else can you use to make your island more interesting?
- Will you have rocks and trees and bushes?
- Is there a cave?
- Where will you bury your treasure to keep it safe from other pirates?
- How will you remember where you left the treasure?

Extend the children's learning by asking them to draw treasure maps with instructions to their crew so that they will be able to find the treasure.

- What kind of secret messages might pirates write to each other?

What children might be learning

✳ to talk about the distinctive features of a treasure island and compare them with their own world

✳ to use positional language to describe where they buried the treasure

✳ to draw maps and write labels.

How children might be learning

✳ by playing in a group, sharing ideas about treasure islands and responding to what other children are saying and doing

✳ by drawing a treasure map, sharing it with others and being proud of what they have achieved

✳ by displaying high levels of motivation and fascination as they return to the activity over the next few days.

Ten Little Pirates by Mike Brownlow and Simon Rickerty (Orchard Books, 2014)

Dinosaur bones

Extra things to collect or make

🔆 Dinosaur Bones Discovery Set or Dinosaur Skulls Set (both available from Yellow Door)

🔆 Boxes or trays of soil or sand deep enough to bury the bones in

🔆 Small brushes, such as paintbrushes, toothbrushes and nailbrushes

🔆 Discovery toolkit: small trowels, seed trays and sieves

🔆 Recording toolkit: string to measure with, paper, pencils, pens, clipboards.

Setting the scene

Encourage a fascination with dinosaurs. Read dinosaur books, find pictures and information online and/or visit a museum.

Bury the bones in boxes or deep trays in the mud kitchen. Set the scene: people who study dinosaurs and fossils are called palaeontologists, a dinosaur dig is called an excavation, and discovered bones need to be measured, recorded and identified.

Send your young palaeontologists out to excavate!

- What kind of dinosaur bones do you think you have discovered?
- How can you identify them?
- What measurements have you made?
- How are the bones different from each other?

Extend the play by turning your mud kitchen into a museum. Freshly dug bones, fossils and stones can be displayed and labelled. There is scope for further role play if the newspapers or television news are interested in reports of particularly spectacular discoveries!

What children might be learning

🔆 to find out information about dinosaurs and how their remains are discovered

🔆 to use and apply new vocabulary about dinosaurs and fossils

🔆 to use their writing skills to make labels and notices for their museum.

How children might be learning

🔆 by looking in detail at non-fiction books in order to become a dinosaur expert

🔆 by being challenged to use new and specific vocabulary about dinosaurs and fossils

🔆 by understanding that writing labels for the museum can give information to others.

Dinosaur Bones by Bob Barner (Chronicle Books, 2001)

The bubbling swamp

Extra things to collect or make

* Deep tray
* Cornflour and bicarbonate of soda
* Small squeezy bottles filled with vinegar
* Set of different-sized spoons.

Setting the scene

Give the children cornflour, soil and water and let them explore how mixing these ingredients together makes a new, gloopy material. Encourage the children to describe what they have made.

Provide bicarbonate of soda to mix into the muddy gloop, followed by vinegar. The children will have created a bubbling swamp! Ask them:

* What other materials might you add?
* What might live in the swamp?
* What can you feel/see/smell?

Extend the children's learning by reading *One Duck Stuck*. Ask the children to identify all the words that describe the mud, such as slimy, squishy, swampy, sticky, soggy, slippy and sloppy.

Ask the children to suggest more words to describe their bubbling swamp. Use this language to make a chant or song with the children for wading through swamps. Add musical percussion and movement as you whisper, shout or sing.

What children might be learning

* to observe and describe what happens when they mix different ingredients together to make a bubbling swamp
* to use alliteration, rhythm and rhyme when describing the bubbling swamp
* to use quiet/loud voices and slow/fast sounds when creating their swampy chants and songs.

How children might be learning

* by being willing to join in and mix ingredients together to make a swamp
* by contributing ideas and listening to the ideas of others
* by being creative, using words and music in their swamp songs and chants.

One Duck Stuck by Phyllis Root and Jane Chapman (Walker Books, 1999)

Mud

Extra things to collect or make

* Images of barefooted people walking in mud
* Yellow roses
* Rose bush
* Muddy area
* Bowls of water
* Soap
* Towels.

Setting the scene

Read 'Mud' to the children and share the images of barefooted people walking in mud, asking:

* Have you felt mud between your toes?
* What did it feel like?
* Why do you think that the rose bush in the poem knows how mud feels between toes?

Bring in some yellow roses for the children to look at and let them smell their scent.

Plant a rose bush in the outdoor area.

Prepare a muddy area for the children to walk in barefooted. Discuss how to keep safe before allowing the children to take off their shoes and socks and feel the mud between their toes.

Extend the children's vocabulary by using words such as wade, squishy, squashy, wiggly. Ask them to recall the poem. Encourage the children to make up their own nonsense words.

Fill bowls with warm, soapy water and provide some towels so

that the children can wash and dry their feet. Discuss how easy/difficult it is to clean the mud from their feet.

Extend the activity by exploring other materials with bare feet, such as wet sand, shaving foam, gravel, sandpaper, cotton wool, and so on.

What children might be learning

* to use appropriate vocabulary to describe the feeling of mud between their toes
* to clean themselves up after getting their feet muddy
* to share in exciting experiences with their friends.

How children might be learning

* by being willing to take off their socks and shoes and feel the squidgy mud between their toes
* by being supported and encouraged by an adult to get dirty and then get clean
* by trying out new experiences and understanding how to keep safe.

Mud by Mary Lyn Ray and Lauren Stringer (Harcourt Brace International, 2001)

The poem 'Mud' by Polly Chase Boyden, which can be found at www.letthechildrenplay.net/2011/06/celebrating-joys-of-mud-play-in.html

Mud families

Extra things to collect or make

✳ Quick-dry clay or wet molehill soil
✳ Pictures of clay pots and sculptures
✳ Clay-modelling tools or matchsticks.

Setting the scene

Read *Mud Family* to yourself first as you might feel it is a story more suitable for older children.

Introduce the story by explaining that it is set a long time ago. Talk with the children about hot countries and explain that sometimes in such places it does not rain for a long time and everything dries out. You might wish to explore some of the personal, social and emotional issues that occur in the story, such as why Sosi's family is hot, tired and cross.

Allow the children time to explore the quick-drying clay or molehill soil. Show them pictures of items made from clay, such as pots and sculptures. Teach the children how to mould the clay and keep it moist, then challenge them to make a pot and/or a mud family like Sosi's.

Encourage the children to use the modelling tools to carve features out of the clay to animate their mud family, discussing what might happen if their mud family is left in the sunshine.

End by allowing the children to make up their own mud family rain dance.

What children might be learning

✳ to talk about how Sosi's environment and experiences might be different from their own
✳ to consider how Sosi was feeling at different points during the story
✳ to use clay, mud and the appropriate tools to plan and make a mud family.

How children might be learning

✳ by exploring feelings and actions through practical responses to a story
✳ by using the clay, tools and techniques they have been taught to make a mud family
✳ by being proud of what they have made.

Mud Family by Betsy James and Paul Morin (San Val, 1998)

One potato, two potato

Extra things to collect or make

* Space to grow potatoes: school allotment, gardening area, large containers
* Seed potatoes (First Early varieties – new potatoes – need to be planted in January/February. Harvest in June/July)
* Weighing scales
* Vegetable boxes.

Setting the scene

Help the children to find out about how to grow potatoes. Can they tell you what they will need to grow potatoes and how to plant them?

When it comes to growing your own potatoes, you need to start the seed potatoes growing out of the soil so that they produce some shoots. Make a potato diary with the children and encourage them to record how the potatoes grow through drawings, photographs and early writing.

Teach the children the counting rhyme 'One Potato, Two Potato' and invent some actions, or play a circle game that goes with the rhyme.

Buy some baking potatoes to scrub, cook and eat with the children. The children might investigate other ways of cooking potatoes, which can be tried and the results tasted and compared, with favourites chosen.

Harvest your own potatoes and cook them. They will taste the best ever!

Make mud potatoes of different sizes in the mud kitchen. The children might explore how many fit in the different vegetable boxes you have collected. Direct them to use weighing scales to compare the weight of different mud potatoes. Use real potatoes in the mud kitchen, planting them, harvesting them and cooking them in the mud oven.

What children might be learning

* to develop an understanding of how potatoes grow
* to record the growth of potato plants over a period of time
* to use weighing scales to compare the weight of mud potatoes and real potatoes.

How children might be learning

* by continuing to be interested in how their potatoes grow over a period of time
* by using weighing scales with care and accuracy
* by exploring and testing the different ways that potatoes can be cooked.

Potatoes by Claire Llewellyn (Franklin Watts, 2003)

Details about growing potatoes can be found at www.rhs.org.uk/advice/grow-your-own/vegetables/potatoes

Slimy mud

Extra things to collect or make

* Green seed trays
* Ingredients: hair gel, shaving foam, soap flakes, cornflour
* Empty snail shells
* Additional materials: cooked spaghetti or noodles.

Setting the scene

Read *The Slimy Book* to the children and allow them to enjoy the rich, descriptive language. Can they think of anything else that is slimy?

Provide a range of ingredients in the mud kitchen for the children to experiment with, asking them:

- Who can make the slimiest mixture?
- What did you use in your mixture?
- Does your mixture have a name?
- Does your mixture remind you of anything from the book?
- What else could you add to the slime?

Adding cooked spaghetti, for example, might make the children think of the worms in the story.

Allow the children to use empty snail shells to make trails in the slime, using words from the story to describe what they have done.

What children might be learning

* to use imaginative vocabulary to describe the physical activity of making and mixing slimy ingredients
* to talk with others about what they have made
* to explore their senses by using different ingredients to make slime.

How children might be learning

* by using their senses to explore the slimy mixture
* by engaging for a sustained period in an open-ended activity
* by being willing to engage with messy materials in a safe way.

The Slimy Book by Babette Cole (Red Fox, 2003)

Mud, mud, glorious mud

Extra things to collect or make

- Pictures and photographs of hippopotami
- Small-world toy animals, such as hippopotami and elephants.

Setting the scene

If possible, take the children to visit a zoo to see hippopotami, otherwise share pictures, photographs and video clips of them instead. Explain that the word 'hippopotamus' means 'water or river horse'. Use non-fiction books to discover:

- How big is a hippopotamus?
- Where do hippopotami live?
- What do they like to eat?
- What is their skin like?
- Can hippopotami float?
- How do they move in water?

Investigate and talk about other creatures that need mud, such as elephants, pigs, mud skippers, mud crabs, mud-flat birds (waders).

Talk about why mud flats are so important to wader birds, discussing how such birds spend their time searching for food, building nests, raising their young and exploring their habitat.

Teach the children The Hippopotamus Song (Mud, Mud, Glorious Mud).

Help the children to set up a muddy small-world scenario outside. Ask the children to estimate how much water they will need to add to the soil to make the mud just the right consistency for their hippopotami.

Discuss what they might add to the mud to recreate the habitat they have seen in pictures/photographs of where hippopotami live. Suggestions might include branches, twigs, grass and plants.

Allow the children to recreate the stories they have heard and sing the song they have learned as they play with the hippopotami.

What children might be learning

- to make observations of animals and find out how they live
- to sing The Hippopotamus Song and add it to their repertoire
- to use what they know about hippopotami and other mud-loving creatures to create a small-world scene and tell stories to and with their peers.

How children might be learning

- by remembering the lyrics and tune of The Hippopotamus Song
- by applying what they know about hippopotami and other mud-loving creatures in their play
- by talking knowledgably about the animals that live on mud flats.

Hot Hippo by Mwenye Hadithi and Adrienne Kennaway (Hodder Children's Books, 1986)

Listen to The Hippopotamus Song (Mud, Mud, Glorious Mud) at www.youtube.com/watch?v=1QW85kfakJcweblinks

The Three Little Pigs

Extra things to collect or make

* Sand
* Dry grass or hay
* Range of sticks
* Images of mud houses from around the world
* Margarine tubs or the base of milk cartons
* Jugs of water
* Sticks / wooden spoons for mixing.

Setting the scene

Tell the story of the three little pigs and encourage the children to join in with the refrains.

Work with the children to make a house of straw and a house of sticks in the outdoor area.

Share pictures of mud houses from around the world and talk about how mud bricks are made. You might want to extend this with older children by exploring the history of house building using bricks and mud.

Teach the children how to make a mud brick using mud, sand, dry grass or hay and water in the mud kitchen. Show the children how to use the tubs as moulds for their bricks. Allow the children to make their own mud bricks, asking:

* What consistency of mud do you think you will need to make a good brick?
* How long will it take for the bricks to dry out? (If needed, explain that it might take a little while for this to happen.)
* Where will you put the bricks to dry?

* How many bricks do you think you will need to make the little pig's house?

When the bricks are dry, support the children as they build model mud houses with the bricks.

What children might be learning

* to mix different materials together to make a mud brick and talk about what they chose and why
* to understand that there are people around the world who live in mud houses
* to explore ideas about building with the mud bricks they have made.

How children might be learning

* by persevering through the process of brick making
* by being confident to try out their own ideas when building a structure
* by working in a team to make enough mud bricks for a structure.

The Three Little Pigs by Heather Amery and Stephen Cartwright (Usborne Publishing, 2003)

Meg and Mog

Extra things to collect or make

* Small cauldrons (you can buy these at Halloween or via the Internet)
* Sticks for stirring
* Homemade hats for witches and wizards.

Setting the scene

Make a display of Meg and Mog books in your book area and share the books with the children in small groups. Talk with the children about witches and wizards, emphasising that they are characters in stories and are not real. Some children may have experienced Halloween and be willing to share their experiences with the group. Be aware that some children may be anxious about witches and wizards and will need some reassurance.

Talk with the children about Meg's breakfast, asking:

* What do you have for breakfast?
* Do you think Mog would like to eat the breakfast that Meg cooked?
* What might she have preferred?

Have a breakfast morning and invite the children and their families to share breakfast before the day begins.

Ask the children to create mud-kitchen breakfasts for Meg. This might be something like the following:

* Three eggs: three pine cones
* Slices of bread: pieces of wood
* Cup of cocoa: cup of dry soil

* A kipper: strip of bark
* Jam: pot of wet mud.

Stir it all up in a cauldron and serve it up!

Ask the children to create some friendly magic spells like Meg's.

What children might be learning

* to talk about breakfast, having heard *Meg and Mog*, recognising that other children's experiences will be different
* to appreciate that Meg and Mog are imaginary characters in books and on television
* to use their imagination by mixing available resources to make Meg's breakfast.

How children might be learning

* by being interested in the ideas and experiences of other children
* by selecting and combining different materials to make breakfast
* by using the mud kitchen to role play the story of Meg and Mog.

Meg and Mog by Helen Nicoll and Jan Pieńkowski (Puffin Books, 2004)
See other Meg and Mog books in the series

Bog Baby

Extra things to collect or make

* Ingredients for uncooked play dough: 1 cup salt, 1 cup water, 2 cups flour, food colouring
* Googly eyes
* Bucket, old tin bath or old sink
* Pond-dipping creature identification sheet (available from www.naturedetectives.org.uk)

Setting the scene

Read *Bog Baby* to the children. There will be lots to talk about!

You might want to make your own 'magic pond' in a bucket, an old sink or tin bath in the outdoor area.

Talk with the children about other creatures that live in ponds, such as frogs, pond skaters, water snails, water beetles, newts, water boatmen, caddisfly larvae, and so on. You could take the children pond dipping elsewhere. It will take some time for a variety of creatures to find your newly-created pond.

Make some uncooked play dough in the mud kitchen. Can the children make a Bog Baby? Give them some googly eyes and let them collect natural materials, such as twigs, leaves and feathers, to use for arms or hair. Has your Bog Baby got a name? Can you make a new story for your Bog Baby? Examples being:

* Bog Baby Goes Camping
* Bog Baby on a Boat Trip on the River
* Bog Baby Lost in the Woods
* Bog Baby at the Restaurant
* Bog Baby Goes Shopping.

What children might be learning

* to use an identification sheet to talk about some of the animals that live in ponds
* to use play dough and other materials to create a Bog Baby
* to use their imagination to make up more adventures for Bog Baby.

How children might be learning

* by using what they know about animals to create imaginative bog babies and other creatures
* by reading an identification sheet to gain information about pond creatures
* by extending their interest in the story to create more adventures for Bog Baby.

The Bog Baby by Jeanne Willis and Gwen Millward (Puffin Books, 2008)

Duck in the Truck

Extra things to collect or make

* Collection of books by Jez Alborough, including *Duck in the Truck*
* Small-world vehicles: cars, trucks
* Ramps
* Outdoor ride-on-vehicles
* Lengths of rope
* Planks of wood
* Car-wash resources: buckets, sponges, washing-up liquid, cloths.

Setting the scene

Make a collection of Jez Alborough books and talk about the author. Read *Duck in the Truck* and ask the children to help you to plan a small-world scene using, soil, ramps, small cars and trucks.

Create a muddy area outside. The children will have fun helping to do this with buckets of water!

Use the ride-on-vehicles, encouraging the children to drive them through the mud. Talk with the children about the tyre tracks that they have created and the patterns that they can see.

Ask the children to remember the story of the duck in the truck.

* What was the duck's problem?
* How did he get the truck out of the mud?
* What might you do if your car/truck gets stuck?

Use rope and planks to rescue a ride-on-car from a muddy puddle.

Make the mud kitchen into a car wash. Can the children take turns to do different jobs? How clean can they make the vehicles?

What children might be learning

* to retell the story of *Duck in the Truck* using small-world resources and through role play
* to wheel their vehicles through the muddy puddle safely and with control
* to work with others to take on different roles in the car wash.

How children might be learning

* by taking on a role from *Duck in the Truck*
* by riding the vehicles through the muddy puddle in a way that is safe and considerate
* by being willing to have a go at driving through the mud and washing the cars.

Duck in the Truck by Jez Alborough (Walker Books, 2004)

Gruffalo stew

Extra things to collect or make

* Paper and felt-tip pens
* Large pan or wok
* Soft-toy Gruffalo or mouse
* Kitchen timer
* Dinosaur Bones Match and Measure Set (Available from Yellow Door).

Setting the scene

Read *The Gruffalo* to the children several times so that they become familiar with it. Encourage the children to join in with the refrains. Talk about the story by asking:

* What do you think a Gruffalo might like to eat?
* What is a stew?
* What might go in a stew?

Build a Gruffalo's den near your mud kitchen. Help the children to make a 'Gruffalo's Kitchen' sign.

Ask the children to make their own Gruffalo stew.

* What will you collect to put in the Gruffalo stew?
* What size bones will you put in?
* How long will you cook the stew for?

Let the children take photographs of their stews and make a book of Gruffalo stew recipes to display in the Gruffalo's den.

What children might be learning

* to join in with the refrains in *The Gruffalo* and anticipate the key events and phrases
* to talk about the characters in *The Gruffalo* and use their play in the mud kitchen to extend the story
* to measure and compare the size of the bones in the Gruffalo stew.

How children might be learning

* by using the ideas from a favourite story in their play
* by trying out their own ideas while making Gruffalo Stew
* by recording what they have done by taking photographs and making a recipe book.

The Gruffalo by Julia Donaldson and Alex Scheffler (Macmillan Children's Books, 1999)

Faces in the trees

Extra things to collect or make

✳ Soil (molehill soil has a good consistency)

✳ Modelling clay

✳ Foliage and blooms from the garden

✳ Pictures of faces from magazines, art postcards, photographs, including images of the Green Man

✳ Mirrors.

Setting the scene

Give each of the children a mirror and ask them to explore their face, supporting them by asking:

- What shape is your nose?
- Can you see your ears or are they covered by your hair?
- Have you got any dimples? They might appear when you smile!
- Can you use your finger to feel the shape of your eyebrows?

Provide resources for the children to draw or paint pictures of their faces.

Now explore a wide range of pictures of faces collected from magazines and art postcards – Arcimboldo's paintings and photographs/images of the Green Man might be of particular interest.

Move your mud kitchen, if needed, nearer to some trees, a fence, shed or playhouse wall. Help the children to collect some foliage and blooms from your outdoor space. Talk with the children about the shapes and smells of the leaves and flowers, while they make their faces.

- What might you use for eyes?
- What are you going to use the leaves for?
- I wonder what you will use for a mouth.

Encourage the children to mould the wet soil or the clay into face shapes and use the natural resources to make the features. Display the faces by pressing them into the tree trunks or wooden surfaces nearby.

Try this activity at different times of the year using seasonal materials. Compare the different faces.

What children might be learning

✳ to explore and use some new vocabulary to describe their own faces

✳ to appreciate that over time artists have represented faces in many different ways

✳ to design and create mud faces and to exhibit them on trees.

How children might be learning

✳ by having extended time to study their own faces and those that are depicted in art

✳ by being encouraged to be creative and to use ideas from different sources when designing their mud faces

✳ by evaluating what they have made and feeling proud of their achievements.

Arcimboldo: Sticker Art Shapes (Frances Lincoln Children's Books, 2008)

The Internet provides a wealth of images of Arcimboldo's paintings and images of the Green Man

Superhero salad

Extra things to collect or make

* Salad bowls and salad servers
* Pictures/photographs of different salads
* Recipes for simple salads using the ingredients below
* Herbs, root ginger, lemon
* Food colouring
* Small jugs.

Setting the scene

All superheroes need to eat! But what do they like to eat?

They definitely need to eat super foods to make sure that their super powers get stronger. Ask the children what super foods they might eat, along with which foods help us to stay strong and healthy.

Encourage the children to taste some superhero food at snack time, such as lettuce, tomato, cucumber, carrot, avocado, celery, radish, broad beans, cress, and so on. Look at recipes for different salads and help the children to make some to share with their families and friends at a superhero lunch.

Outside in the superhero mud kitchen, collect ingredients from the outdoor space – leaves, grass, petals, pebbles – to make imaginative superhero salads. Do not forget to fill the jugs with tasty salad dressings using water, herbs, ginger, lemon and food colouring. Dribble the salad dressings over the superhero salads for extra powers.

Encourage more imaginative thinking:

* What else could you make for superheroes to eat?
* What might they like to drink?

What children might be learning

* to read words and simple sentences when following a salad recipe
* to appreciate that eating a good variety of salads can contribute to a healthy lifestyle
* to experiment with ideas about the foods that might be enjoyed by superheroes with different powers.

How children might be learning

* by knowing about some of the foods that contribute to a healthy diet
* by using their phonic knowledge to decode regular words when reading salad recipes
* by being a thinker as they create their superhero salads.

Super Daisy and the Peril of Planet Pea by Kes Gray and Nick Sharratt (Red Fox, 2009)
Come Alive Superheroes Resource Pack by Helen Bromley (Yellow Door, 2010)

Have a cup of tea at the builders' mud café

Extra things to collect or make

✳ Selection of tea bags, both herbal and non-herbal
✳ Camping kettle, enamel tin mugs and teaspoons
✳ Self-fill tea bags
✳ Bowls (for sugar)
✳ Cornflour
✳ Plastic bottles
✳ Quick-dry clay
✳ Cookie cutters.

Setting the scene

Let the children explore a selection of tea bags.

- Who likes tea?
- Where is tea grown?
- How do you make tea?
- Have you ever tried herbal tea?

Let the children smell the herbal tea bags. Model vocabulary, such as spicy, sweet, fruity, aromatic and minty.

Make several types of herbal tea, let them cool and allow the children to taste a little of each one. Ask them which flavour they liked the best and why.

This can evolve to become part of the following role play:

The builders outside are in need of a break from their work. Open the Builders' Mud Café and make cups of tea to quench their thirst. Make some 'milk' using water and cornflour, decant it into bottles and put them in the mud-kitchen fridge. Put some grass, leaves, petals and herbs into the self-fill tea bags and

place these in the mugs. Use water from the camping kettle to fill the mugs, add milk and then offer the builders some sugar (dry mud) with their tea, should they want some.

Roll out the quick dry-clay and use the cookie cutters to make some biscuits. These can be decorated with natural resources from the outdoor space. A further discussion might be had about whether a lot of sugar in tea and biscuits is good for you.

What children might be learning

✳ to use a sequence of actions to make a cup of tea
✳ to use new vocabulary to describe the smell, look and taste of different teas
✳ to socialise with others as they have their tea in the mud kitchen.

How children might be learning

✳ by using their senses when they explore making and tasting tea
✳ by taking on a role in the mud café
✳ by playing in a group to extend and invent ideas in the mud café.

Books relating to the television series *Bob the Builder*

Muddy footballers

Extra things to collect or make

* Range of football shirts
* Seed trays or shoe-box lids lined with plastic
* Photographs, books and magazines about football
* Three-minute timer
* Whistle
* Football
* Photographs of children wearing football strip, laminated and attached to a peg, or wooden football characters (Come Alive Football Characters are available from Yellow Door).

Setting the scene

A familiar scene from across the world when a football season is underway involves children asking:

* Can we play football?
* Can we set up some goals?
* Which team do you support?
* Where do they play?
* What are your team's colours?

Make sure that there are non-fiction books, football magazines and old football match programmes available to meet this interest.

Turn the mud kitchen into a food stand at a football stadium. Make drinks, pies and soup for half time. Use a three-minute timer and play the first half of the game, with a child as the referee, who blows a whistle to stop play. After refreshments from the food stand, the teams may play the second half.

Talk about looking after the football pitch and, if possible, visit your local stadium. Sow some grass seed in seed trays or lined shoe-box lids filled with compost to create mini football pitches, exploring:

* What grass seed needs to grow
* Whether the grass is growing evenly
* How the grass might be cut.

Once their pitch has grown, they can paint on some pitch markings, make two goals and, using a small ball and some football characters, play a miniature match. Allow the children to record the goals on a whiteboard.

What children might be learning

* to describe and explain what they know about playing football to their friends
* to relate their own experiences of football to their play in the mud kitchen
* to explain what grass seed needs to grow.

How children might be learning

* by being excited about following their interest in football through activities in the mud kitchen
* by sharing their ideas and knowledge with their friends
* by being patient and focused over a period of time as the grass of their football pitch grows.

First Sticker Book: Football by Sam Taplin and Annalisa Sanmartino (Usbourne Publishing, 2013)

Football match programmes
Magazines about football

Muddy invertebrates (minibeasts)

Extra things to collect or make

* Collecting resources: hand lenses, small pots, teaspoons
* Minibeast identification cards or reference books
* Set of plastic or stone invertebrates (both available from Yellow Door)
* Resources for minibeast inventions: clay, twigs, leaves, small stones, petals
* Camera.

Setting the scene

Take the children outside to hunt for invertebrates. Look at them carefully using hand lenses.

Support the children to identify what they find.

Look for invertebrates in different places.

* I wonder what likes to visit flowers and what lives in dead leaves.

Use a good set of plastic invertebrates to look at the features of different animals. Ask the children to sort them, using their observational skills to think about:

* How many have wings?
* How many have six legs?
* What shape bodies do they have?
* What kinds of colours and patterns do they show?

Introduce and model specific vocabulary to describe the features of invertebrates.

Explain to the children that the mud kitchen has become an inventors' invertebrate workshop. Ask them to use clay and other

materials to invent and make invertebrates. Encourage them to reflect on their models.

* Have you added legs/wings/jaws/antennae?
* What about camouflage?
* Have you invented names for your animals?

Ask the children to take photographs of their models to use in an invertebrate identification poster or book.

What children might be learning

* to use an identification sheet to find out information about invertebrates
* to use clay and other materials to create a fantasy invertebrate
* to use specific vocabulary to describe invertebrates and their behaviour.

How children might be learning

* by using what they know about invertebrates to create fantasy creatures
* by knowing that they can use non-fiction materials to help them to learn new information
* by being curious about how invertebrates behave.

Let's Look for Minibeasts by Caz Buckingham and Andrea Pinnington (Fine Feather Press, 2015)

Magical mud

Extra things to collect or make

* Cake tins, bun tins, pie dishes
* Large bowl
* Sticks and/or wooden spoons for mixing
* Bicarbonate of soda
* Powder paints
* Jug of vinegar.

Setting the scene

Let the children enjoy making mud cakes, buns and pies in the mud kitchen, but this time add a good amount of bicarbonate of soda to the mud and let the children continue mixing and making.

- How many buns have you made?
- I wonder if you can make one more.
- That's a huge pie! Maybe you can make one that is even bigger.

Let the children use the powder paints to decorate their creations. Talk about the colours available and let them experiment with mixing the colours.

Finally, give the children the jug of vinegar. Before pouring it over their creations, explain:

- Let's investigate what will happen when you pour the vinegar onto your colourful cakes, buns and pies.

The children will love watching their bakes erupt into rainbows of colour. Let them add more vinegar until the reaction stops. Discuss what happened and then have a go at turning the mud kitchen into a bubbling swamp (see page 34).

What children might be learning

* to observe and describe what happens when they mix different ingredients together to make magical mud
* to count cakes, buns and pies and to use the language of addition and subtraction
* to talk about and describe what they are doing and what they can see happening.

How children might be learning

* by being willing to join in and mix ingredients together to make magical mud
* by contributing ideas and listening to the ideas of others
* by being confident about using mathematical ideas in their play.

Mud Pie Annie by Sue Buchanan, Dana Shafer and Joy Allen (Zondervan, 2008)

Mud kitchen princesses

Extra things to collect or make

* Paper and felt-tip pens
* Metal pie dishes
* Glitter gems, sparkly jewels, glitter, sequins, shiny coloured stones
* Dressing-up clothes
* Powder paint
* Food colouring
* Essential oils, such as lavender
* Unscented shaving foam
* Icing bags and nozzles
* Flowers, petals.

Setting the scene

Extend any daily princess role-play by transforming the mud kitchen into a place fit for royalty. Help the children to make and decorate some paper bunting to hang up in the mud kitchen and then stock it with pots of glittery jewels, sequins and gems.

Let the children dress up in character. Encourage them to enjoy the sensory experience of mixing dry soil and water, adding different aromatics and art materials to make a princess pie.

Teach the children how to use an icing bag, filling it with a mixture of shaving foam, food colouring and a few drops of lavender oil, asking them:

* What icing pattern are you going to decorate your pie with?
* What other things are you going to use to decorate your pie?

Use a slate board to write a menu of princess pies: Sparkly Pie, Glitter Pie, Lavender Pie, and so on.

What children might be learning

* to contribute their ideas and listen to those of others in order to transform the mud kitchen into a magical place
* to experiment with different media to design and make sparkly princess pies
* to write for a purpose as they create a menu of princess pies.

How children might be learning

* by working together to decide what resources to add to the mud kitchen
* by being supported by an adult to use their phonic knowledge to write menus
* by trying out their ideas when creating princess pies.

I Don't Want to Wash my Hands (A Little Princess Story) by Tony Ross (Andersen, 2012)

Mud kitchen wizards

Extra things to collect or make

- ❋ Fresh herbs: coriander, basil, mint, rosemary
- ❋ Seed trays/flower pots
- ❋ Compost
- ❋ Watering cans
- ❋ Herb seeds that can be grown outdoors: parsley, chives, rosemary, coriander, dill
- ❋ Sticks
- ❋ Potato peelers
- ❋ Decorative materials: raffia, string, wool, ribbons, leaves, feathers, plus felt-tip pens.

Setting the scene

Show the children some fresh herbs and allow them to touch, smell and taste them. Engage the children in conversation by naming the herbs and wondering what they are used for. Can the children guess how and where the herbs grow?

Suggest that the children grow some herbs to use in their mud kitchen recipes. Teach them how to fill the seed trays with compost and plant the seeds. As the seeds germinate, they might need to be replanted. Engage the children in conversation by wondering how long it might take for the seeds to grow, and by asking if they can guess what the seeds need to be able to grow.

Place the seed trays on a shelf in the mud kitchen and explain that people sometimes grow herbs on their kitchen window ledges. Monitor their growth and, in time, allow the children to harvest them and use them in the mud kitchen.

Make the activity a little more magical by making magic wands using sticks. Let the children use a potato peeler to carefully scrape the bark off their stick, always pointing the peeler away from themselves. Decorate the wands with raffia, string, wool, ribbons, leaves, feathers and felt-tip pens. Now the children are ready to compose some magic spells to help their herb seeds to grow.

What children might be learning

- ❋ to use the correct vocabulary to talk about herbs and growing
- ❋ to understand the principles of growth and change over time
- ❋ to use their imagination and the resources to hand to create and play with magic wands.

How children might be learning

- ❋ by exploring what happens when they plant seeds and grow herbs
- ❋ by continuing to be interested by how things grow over time
- ❋ by understanding and celebrating their make-believe play with wands.

Walking the World in Wonder: A Children's Herbal by Ellen Evert Hopman and Steven Foster (Healing Arts Press, 2000)
Spells by Emily Gravett (Macmillan Children's Books, 2009)

Magical-mud dragon eggs

Extra things to collect or make

* Small-world toy dragons (Dragon Realm figures are available from Yellow Door)
* Balloons
* Newspaper and tissue paper
* Wallpaper paste
* Natural resources: leaves, petals, grasses.

Setting the scene

Before the children arrive, set up a small-world scenario in the mud kitchen using mud, stones, gravel, plants and dragon figures.

Tell the children that dragons have invaded the mud kitchen! Ask them:

- Where might they have come from?
- What might they want?
- Are they friendly?

The children might want to welcome the dragons by making them some dragon food in the mud kitchen, but nothing too hot, otherwise it will ignite their fiery breath!

Explain that the dragons are looking for their dragon eggs that were all lost one very windy day. Suggest that the children help the dragons by making them some more eggs. Use newspaper and tissue paper dipped in wallpaper paste to cover the balloons. These will need to be left to dry for a couple of days, but in the meantime the children can take care of the dragons and, in turn, the dragons will tell them stories.

When the eggs are dry, tell the children that the dragons like their new eggs but are concerned that they might be taken by predators. Ask the children to camouflage the eggs with natural materials and build nests in the mud kitchen to keep them safe. The children might want to write notices warning others to play quietly and carefully in and near the mud kitchen, so as not to disturb the dragons and their eggs.

What children might be learning

* to use specific vocabulary about how to keep eggs safe from predators, including the use of camouflage
* to respect other creatures and their welfare through imaginative play about dragons
* to plan and make dragon eggs and nests using a variety of tools and materials.

How children might be learning

* by sustaining and developing creative ideas about dragons
* by planning and making decisions about how to create dragon eggs and nests
* by being curious about dragons and how they might be feeling in different situations.

Dragons love Tacos by Adam Rubin and Daniel Salmieri (Dial Books, 2015)
The Egg by M.P. Robertson (Frances Lincoln, 2008)

The aliens are coming

Extra things to collect or make

* Aluminium foil
* Hard hats from the construction area
* Recording of music with a moon or space theme
* Selection of musical instruments
* Decorative materials: bubble wrap, stars, glitter
* Food toppings: hair gel, shaving foam, cornflour
* Quick-dry clay.

Setting the scene

Read *Here Come the Aliens* and discuss the following:

* What are aliens?
* What might they look like?
* Where might they live?
* Are they friendly?

Write down some of the group's ideas about how to look after an alien.

Suggest that the children prepare a feast for the aliens to welcome them to earth. Turn the mud kitchen into a space café by covering it with bubble wrap, stars and glitter. Wrap silver foil around the children's boots and hard hats and play some atmospheric moon music. The children might wish to make their own music.

Discuss what aliens might like to eat. Give some suggestions, such as muddy moonburgers, flying-saucer pizzas, space-critter jelly, juicy rocket fuel or Milky Way smoothies.

The children can use natural resources to make the food, but slimy, shiny ingredients, such as hair gel and glitter, will make it more attractive to aliens!

Write a menu of space food ready for the aliens' arrival.

What children might be learning

* to recognise that not everyone is the same and that people have different likes and dislikes
* to use the sounds of different instruments to make moon music
* to play well with other children as they develop and perform a role play.

How children might be learning

* by understanding that not everyone is the same
* by reviewing their own and other children's moon music and being willing to make changes
* by planning with other children to create role-play stories about aliens.

Here Come the Aliens by Colin McNaughton (Walker Books, 1997)

We hope you have found this publication useful. Further titles in our '50 Exciting ideas' range are:

Builder's Tray	50 Exciting Ways to Use a Builder's Tray	978-1-903670-15-6
Let's Explore!	50 Exciting Starting Points for Science Activities	978-1-903670-11-8
Let's Build	50 Exciting Ideas for Construction Play	978-1-903670-30-9
Let's Take a Story Book Outside	Exciting Ways to Promote Outdoor Creativity	978-1-903670-76-7
Let's Talk Behaviour!	50 Inclusive Ideas to Support Effective Communication and Understanding	978-1-903670-93-4
Let's Write!	50 Exciting Starting Points for Writing Experiences	978-1-903670-10-1
Literacy Outdoors	50 Exciting Starting Points for Outdoor Literacy Experiences	978-1-903670-53-8
Maths Outdoors	50 Exciting Ways to Develop Mathematical Awareness Outdoors	978-1-903670-61-3
Maths Through Stories	50 Exciting Ideas for Developing Maths Through Stories	978-1-903670-46-0
Mud Kitchens and Beyond	50 Exciting Ideas for Investigative Play	978-1-903670-96-5
Nursery Rhymes	50 Nursery Rhymes to Play With	978-1-903670-23-1
Things to Do Outside	50 Exciting Things to Do Outside	978-1-903670-07-1
This is the Way I Like to Play	50 Exciting Ideas to Support Investigative Play through Schemas	978-1-903670-95-8
Plant an Idea	50 Exciting Ways to Use Flowers, Trees and Plant Life Throughout the Year	978-1-903670-24-8
Science Outdoors	50 Exciting Ways for Children to Explore the World Around Them	978-1-903670-67-5
The Small World Recipe Book	50 Exciting Ideas for Small World Play	978-1-903670-39-2
Storyboxes	50 Exciting Ideas for Storyboxes	978-1-903670-16-3
Superheroes and Popular Culture	50 Exciting Ideas for Using Superheroes and Popular Culture	978-1-903670-79-8

Other relevant Lawrence Educational titles include:

Let's Get Talking!	Exciting Ways to Help Children with Speech and Language Difficulties	978-1-903670-88-0
Let's Talk About Maths!	Exciting Ways to Develop Children's Language and Love of Maths From an Early Age	978-1-903670-92-7
On Your Marks!	A Practical Guide to Mark Making, Early Writing and Language	978-1-903670-97-2
Supporting Quiet Children	Exciting Ideas and Activities to Help 'Reluctant Talkers' Become 'Confident Talkers'	978-1-903670-90-3

For further information about these and our other publications, visit our website:
www.LawrenceEducational.co.uk